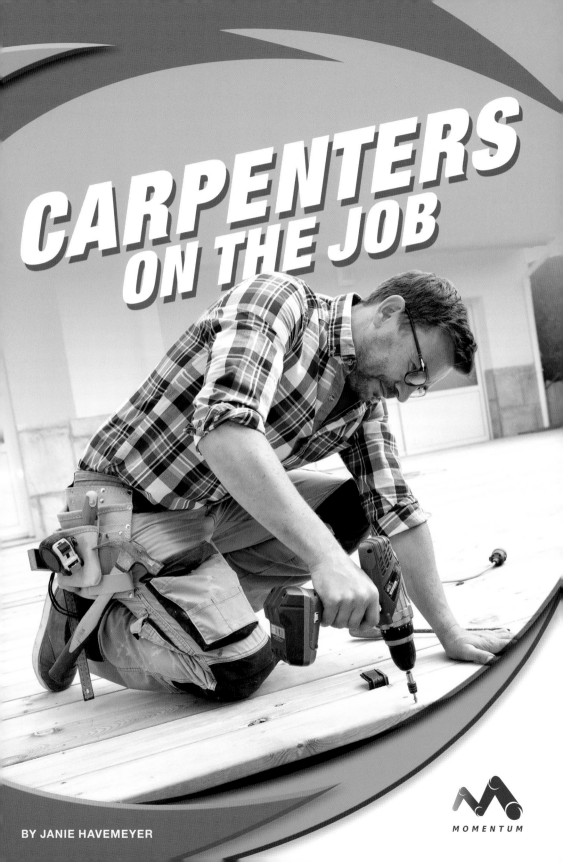

CARPENTERS
ON THE JOB

BY JANIE HAVEMEYER

MOMENTUM

Published by The Child's World®
1980 Lookout Drive • Mankato, MN 56003-1705
800-599-READ • www.childsworld.com

Content Consultant: Leo Lukas, Carpentry
Instructor, Mesabi Range College

Photographs ©: Shutterstock Images, cover, 1,
6, 18, 21, 22, 26; iStockphoto, 5, 14, 15, 17; Steve
Debenport/iStockphoto, 8; Steve Cole Images/
iStockphoto, 9; Andre Koehn/Shutterstock
Images, 10; Brian Goodman/Shutterstock Images,
12; Dragon Images/Shutterstock Images, 20;
Gorma K/Shutterstock Images, 25; Paul Tessier/
Shutterstock Images, 28

ISBN 9781503835474
LCCN 2019942966

Printed in the United States of America

CONTENTS

MOMENTUM

FAST FACTS

What's the Job?

► Carpenters build and repair many things. They build small things such as furniture and bigger things such as houses and bridges. Most carpenters build things out of wood, but they also use other materials such as plastic.

► A carpenter can learn the trade by taking classes and working as an **apprentice** with an experienced carpenter.

► Some of the responsibilities of a carpenter are to read and follow **blueprints**, measure and shape materials such as wood, and put in things such as windows.

Important Stats

► In 2018, the U.S. government estimated that there were 718,730 carpenters in the country.

► In 2018, the average yearly pay for carpenters was $51,120.

► By 2026, the number of carpenters is expected to grow 8 percent.

► California has the highest number of working carpenters.

**Carpenters need to be in good shape. In this ►
line of work, people need to bend, climb,
kneel, and lift heavy materials. They also might
need to work outside in bad weather.**

CHAPTER ONE

THE APPRENTICE

R ick pressed the sharp tip of a metal nail into a wooden plank. He clutched the blue rubber handle of his hammer and brought it crashing down. The hammer hit the nail head. But instead of going into the plank, the nail flew off the wood. It landed on the floor with a *pling*. Rick tried again. This time, he got the nail to lodge into the board. But the next time he hit it, the nail bent to the left. Each time Rick hit the nail, it bent further. He wasn't hitting it correctly. Sometimes, Rick swung at the nail and missed it. Soon, the nail was so bent it looked like a paper clip. He used the claw of the hammer to pry it loose. Rick would have to try again with a new nail. Hammering nails was much harder than it looked.

◄ **Apprentices need to learn the basics of carpentry before moving on to complicated projects.**

▲ Classes can help people learn trade skills.

Rick was an apprentice for an experienced carpenter. He had graduated high school a couple years before and was now taking classes at a local trade school to increase his carpentry skills. In school he was learning about how to stay safe on the job and how to read blueprints. He also studied different carpentry methods and polished up his math skills. Rick knew he would be an apprentice for a few years to learn while on the job. It was important to practice skills in a real work setting.

Blueprints help carpenters get the job done right. ►

During his apprenticeship, Rick fetched and carried materials for the experienced carpenter. He would carry heavy saws and buckets of tools. Often, sweat covered his face and his arms ached. While the experienced carpenter worked, Rick took notes. He was learning a lot by watching. But he also wanted a chance to practice things by himself.

Finally, the carpenter gave Rick an important task. They were working on remodeling a house. A large window at the front of the house needed repair. The carpenter asked Rick to take off the outside window **trim** that framed the window. Rick climbed a ladder so he was standing 16 feet (4.8 m) off the ground. He used a **crowbar** to pry the old boards loose. Finally, when the boards were off, the carpenter came over to look at Rick's work. He slapped Rick on the back and said Rick had done a good job. The time had come to give Rick even more carpentry tasks.

◄ **Crowbars help pry wood loose.**

CHAPTER TWO

FINDING SOLUTIONS

Sean concentrated on the silver blade of the saw. It spun around and around. If he wasn't careful the blade could slice off his finger. The saw wailed when Sean slid the wood through the blade. He guided plank after plank across the blade, cutting boards to be the same length. Sean and the carpenter he was studying under had been hired to rebuild a rotting deck at someone's lake cabin. They had already built the floor, or platform, of the deck. Now, they were working on building a staircase up to the deck. The stairs would have ten steps. The steps were made out of two pieces of wood called the tread and **riser**. The tread was where you placed your foot when you walked up the stairs. Risers were the upright boards between the treads. Each step on the staircase had to be exactly the same measurement.

◄ **Power tools, such as table saws, help carpenters with their projects.**

▲ **Carpenters have to make the right calculations when building with wood.**

Sean had been an apprentice for two years. Over that time, he had become skilled at using sharp tools and noisy table saws. He loved his job. Sean felt that climbing ladders, working outside, and building things was much more fun than sitting in an office.

By the early evening, Sean was cutting the last riser for the top of the staircase. He was moving faster than he had been when he first started cutting wood that day. Sean was ready to move on to the next step. He wore a dust mask to protect his lungs. He also wore goggles to protect his eyes from the wood dust. A thin layer of it clung to his shirt. The spinning blade sliced off a big piece of wood. Sean set the cut board down on top of the others.

▲ **Cutting boards right the first time can save carpenters from issues later on.**

Then, he groaned. The last board was shorter than the others. He had ruined the last piece by making it too short. The carpenter had bought the exact number of boards needed to rebuild the deck. Now, there were no more boards left. Sean couldn't simply cut a new one.

The carpenter Sean was working with noticed his problem. He came over and Sean turned off the saw. There was a solution to the issue, the carpenter said. Sean just needed to figure out what it was.

Sean knew that being a carpenter involved solving many problems. He looked at the pile of scrap wood nearby and chewed on his bottom lip as he thought. Then, Sean realized what he needed to do. One way to make his board longer was to attach another piece to the end. Sean searched among the scraps of cut wood until he found a piece that he liked. He cut **finger joints** into one end of the scrap wood with his saw. He did the same thing to the other board. This took skill and practice. Then, he added glue to the joints and slid the two boards together. The pieces fit tightly together like interlocking hands. The new board was now the perfect length. The carpenter was impressed with Sean's work. The deck would be perfect once it was complete.

**Carpenters can develop a lot of important skills. ►
Some carpenters even know how to make furniture.**

CHAPTER THREE

TRIMMING AND FITTING

Nina MacLaughlin was on her hands and knees in a small closet. She was fitting pieces of wood along the base of the closet. A carpenter puts special pieces of wood at the bottom of a wall to make it look nice. This is called trim work. Each wood piece needs to fit perfectly with the piece next to it. The corner pieces are the hardest to cut. Nina lay on her side with her feet sticking out from the closet. The job would have been easier if the closet wasn't so tiny.

Nina worked with an experienced carpenter, Mary. They were redoing the first floor of an old house built in the 1700s. Old homes like this were not easy to fix up. Nina used the math skills she learned in school to measure wood and cut it down by inches. She was making fewer mistakes now than she had at the start of her apprenticeship. Nina used some tools to get the job done.

◄ **Trim can be placed in many areas, such as around windows, above the floor, and below the ceiling.**

▲ **Electric palm sanders help carpenters smooth wood quickly.**

She used a tape measure, a wood pencil, a saw, and a sander for this task. She walked back and forth from the closet to the garage. She recut pieces of trim, shaved them down, and **sanded** them smooth until they finally fit.

Mary said it would take years to get good at this. But when Nina was finished, Mary gave her a thumbs up. She was getting the hang of carpentry. Nina was proud to be a female carpenter. In 2018, only 2 percent of carpenters were women.

Sanding wood can kick up sawdust, so it's ▶ important that people wear eye protection.

A few weeks later, Mary and Nina were building a kitchen from the ground up. Mary studied the blueprints. She showed Nina where everything would go. Later, she pointed out four pipes in the back stairwell that had to be covered. They rose from the stairs to the ceiling. Mary asked Nina to build a **chase**, or a pipe hider. Go slow and plan ahead, Mary warned. Nina didn't think it would be hard to build a tall, narrow, three-sided box to cover the pipes.

Nina measured and cut the wood. She attached the pieces of wood with glue and nails. Finally, the chase was ready. Nina put all her weight into pressing it against the wall. First, she pressed the top of the chase against the ceiling. Then, she pressed the bottom of the chase against the wall. But something was wrong— the chase wasn't fitting. Nina noticed a small bump on the floor. The chase needed to move over the bump if it was going to press up tightly against the wall. Mary's words about planning ahead rang in Nina's ears. She wished she had noticed the bump earlier.

Nina lifted the chase and carried it outside. She sanded the bottom and then tried to press it in place again. She pushed hard. The chase still wouldn't move over the bump. She sanded off a little more. If she shaved too much away, she would ruin it.

◄ **Construction on a house can be a messy job.**

On the third try, Nina finally got the chase to slide over the bump. At last, all the pipes were covered.

Nina stepped back to look at her work. Then, Mary reminded Nina of the first thing that she should have done. Nina had been so worried about how to get the chase to fit, she had forgotten an important task. Mary had asked her to use a fire spray to cover the holes in the ceiling and floor where the pipes passed. The spray turned into a hard foam that plugged up the empty space. If there was a fire, the spray would slow down the fire's burn. Nina knew how important fire safety was, so she took the chase down again. Nina was feeling impatient, but she had solved all the problems on her own. She took a deep breath and kept on working to get it right.

Some people want to hide pipes in their house ▶ so they don't have to look at them.

25

CHAPTER FOUR

AN EXPERIENCED CARPENTER

Ian looked at the large red barn in front of him. He had been hired to put **shingles** on the roof. His first step was to take measurements. Ian calculated the width and length of the roof. Then, he bought the right amount of shingles and roofing felt. Roofing felt is important. It stops water from leaking inside the building. It's also what the shingles would be nailed onto. Then, Ian got started.

He worked with a team to finish the barn. They climbed to the top of the roof and began rolling out the felt. Ian made sure it was straight and tight. He hammered some nails into the material so it wouldn't move. Then, he started hammering shingles onto the roof. Fields of corn seemed to stretch out in every direction.

Once the wooden roof of the barn was covered in the felt, the team started shingling. The shingles were rough in Ian's hands.

◀ **Working at great heights can be dangerous. People who are roofing need to be aware of their surroundings.**

▲ **Using a nail gun helps keep shingles secure.**

He started at the bottom of the roof and overlapped the shingles as he nailed them down.

Just as the sun started to set, his team climbed down from the barn. They took a step back and looked at their hard work. The roof was complete. The team waved goodbye to each other.

Ian took off his toolbelt and slipped into his truck. The leaves were just starting to change on the trees. Once winter came, Ian would take some time off from official carpentry projects. Work slows down in the cold months. In the spring, more people hire carpenters. But Ian always has plenty of personal carpentry projects to keep his hands busy. He makes new things in his home workshop, such as cabinets and tables. Ian's workshop echoes with hammer bangs every day.

THINK ABOUT IT

► Why is hands-on training such an important part of becoming a carpenter? Can these skills only be learned in a classroom? Why or why not?
► Why is carpentry important?
► What are some of the advantages and disadvantages of not working in an office setting?

GLOSSARY

apprentice (uh-PREN-tis): An apprentice is someone who is learning a trade skill by working with a skilled worker. The apprentice learned carpentry by working with a carpenter.

blueprints (BLOO-prints): Blueprints are detailed plans of how something will be built. The carpenter read the blueprints to see where everything would go in the new kitchen.

chase (CHAYSS): A chase is a box or column that covers house pipes that run from the floor to the ceiling. The chase hid the pipes.

crowbar (KROH-bar): A crowbar is a metal bar used to pry things apart. The carpenter used a crowbar to pry the heavy board loose.

finger joints (FING-gur JOYNTS): Finger joints are joints formed by cutting two board ends into fingerlike shapes that fit together. The carpenter made finger joints to join two pieces of wood together.

riser (RY-zer): A riser is the upright or vertical board between two stair treads. Each step is made of a tread attached to a riser.

sanded (SAND-ed): Something that is sanded has been made smooth by rubbing it with sandpaper or a sanding tool. The carpenter sanded the edge of the board to make it smooth.

shingles (SHING-guhls): Shingles are small pieces of building materials used to cover up roofs. The carpenter hammered the new shingles onto the roof of the house.

trim (TRIM): Trim is material, such as wood, used to decorate windows, doorways, or the base of walls. The carpenter added trim to the windows.

TO LEARN MORE

BOOKS

Larson, Margaret. *Wood Shop: Handy Skills and Creative Building Projects for Kids.* North Adams, MA: Storey Publishing, 2018.

Levete, Sarah. *Maker Projects for Kids Who Love Woodworking.* New York, NY: Crabtree Publishing Company, 2017.

Small, Cathleen. *Carpenter.* New York, NY: Cavendish Square Publishing, 2016.

WEBSITES

Visit our website for links about carpenters: **childsworld.com/links**

Note to Parents, Teachers, and Librarians: We routinely verify our Web links to make sure they are safe and active sites. So encourage your readers to check them out!

SELECTED BIBLIOGRAPHY

Carosso, Juan. *At Your Best As a Carpenter.* New York, NY: Skyhorse Publishing, 2018.

MacLaughlin, Nina. *Hammer Head: The Making of a Carpenter.* New York, NY: W. W. Norton & Company, 2015.

"Occupational Employment and Wages, May 2018." *Bureau of Labor Statistics*, March 29, 2019, bls.gov. Accessed 1 Apr. 2019.

INDEX

ABOUT THE AUTHOR

Janie Havemeyer is an author of many books for young readers. Janie has a master's degree in education and has taught in schools and museums. Janie lives in San Francisco, California.